IOS 8 APP DEVELOPMENT

DEVELOP YOUR OWN APP FAST AND EASY

By Matthew Gimson

Table of Contents

Introduction

iOS 8 is now in the market. There are numerous devices, including mobile phones and tablets, running this version of iOS. These devices need to have apps that their users will enjoy using. This is why you should learn how to develop these apps. Swift is the programming language that was released for developing iOS 8 apps. This book will guide you in developing your own iOS apps.

Chapter 1- Definition

iOS is a mobile operating system developed and used by Apple Inc. iOS 8 is the eight version of this operating system, and it was released as a successor to iOS 7. The release of iOS 8 was announced at the World Wide Developer's Conference (WWDC) 2014 on June 2, 2014. It was seen as the greatest change brought to iOS operating system since its release, and its features are closely related to those of iOS 7, as it is an improvement of the features of the latter. Most of the changes introduced in version 8 were aimed at improving and enhancing the features of the interface. By August 2015, iOS 8 had been installed in over 86% of Apple devices. Currently, its latest version is iOS 8.4.1, and it was released in August 2015.

When iOS 8 was introduced, a programming language, named Swift, was also introduced. Swift is the programming language used to develop apps that will run on iOS 8. Apple also developed the programming language. The language combines the features of both C and Objective-C programming languages, but the compatibility constraints of C programming language were not imported into this programming language. Note that apps developed in Swift can also run in the other versions of the iOS operating system, such as iOS 6 and others.

Chapter 2- Getting Started

Before you can begin programing in Swift, you must identify and set up the environment you intend to use for this purpose. For those who are not interested in setting up the environment locally, you can choose to use the environments that are provided online free of charge. The experience will be similar.

However, for those of you who need to set up the environment locally, this can easily be done, and the language provides an interesting playground in which you can write your code. However, make sure that you have downloaded the xCode software.

My assumption is that you have set up your own account with the Apple Developer website. Once you have done this, login to your account and then click the link "Download for Apple Developers." After clicking the above link, all the software available for free download will be listed.

 Developer   Technologies   Resources

Downloads for Apple Developers

You can then select the xCode and then click on the link next to the disc image to download it. The process of downloading the "dmg" file will continue and finally, it will complete. Once it completes, double click on it to begin the installation process. You should then follow the onscreen instructions that will be presented to you. Once you are done, the xCode icon can then be dropped into the folder for "Applications."

Xcode   Applications

With the above, the xCode will be set up in your system, so you will be ready to get started with Swift programming. You can now open the "Applications" folder and then click on the xCode icon. Accept the terms and conditions, and the app will open.

You can then select the option "Get started with a playground" and then provide the name for the playground. You should also select "iOS" as the platform. From now on, any program that you write in xCode should have "import Cocoa." The app comes with the following default code:

import UIKit

var str = "Hello, playground"

Our Test program

The test program for Swift should be written as follows:

import Cocoa

/* Our Hello program in Swift */

var string = "Hello, there!"

println(string)

You can write, and then run the above program. You will observe the following output:

```
Hello, there!
```

As shown in the program, the "import Cocoa" statement was used to import the program to your environment. If you are writing the same program for the iOS playground, then the "UIKit" should be imported as shown below:

import UIKit

var string = "Hello, there!"

println(string)

The program will give you the same output as the previous one.

Chapter 3- The Basic Syntax in Swift

So far, you have learned some of the basic constructs that can be used in Swift. Some of the other syntaxes that are used in Swift are discussed below.

Tokens in Swift

In Swift, there are various tokens. The token in this case can be a constant, an identifier, a symbol, a string literal, or a keyword. Consider the example given below:

println("A test program!")

The tokens include the following:

println

(
"A test!"
)

Comments

Whenever the compiler encounters a comment in Swift, it ignores it. They act as a helping text in your program. For the case of multiline comments, they should begin with the symbol "/*" and then terminate with the symbol "*/". Consider the example given below:

/* This is a comment in swift */
Swift also supports nesting of multi-line comments. Consider the example given below:

/* This is the first line the swift comment
/* this is the second line of the swift comment. */

If you are using a single line comment in swift, then denote it by use of the symbol "//" as shown below:
// This is a single line comment in Swift

Note that in Swift, the use of the semicolon at the end of your statements is not mandatory. However, if you use it, it will be okay you will not get an error.

However, for those who like to use multiple statements in a single line, then a semicolon is mandatory since it will act as a delimiter. If you fail to do this, a syntax error will be produced. Consider the example given below:

import Cocoa

/* A program in swift */

var string = "Hello, there!"; println(string)

As shown in the program, the two last lines of the program were written in a single line. After running the program, you will get the following output:

```
Hello, there!
```

Chapter 4- Data Types in Swift

For programming to be effective, you have to use variables to store values. Variables mean a memory location that is reserved. However, you need to know that variables are of various data types, and this means that different amounts of memory spaces are reserved for them. In Swift the basic data types that are supported include: integers, double, float, characters, string, Boolean, and Optional.

Type Aliases

You can use the "typealias" to create a new name for a type that already exists. Consider the example given below showing how a simple alias can be created in Swift:

typealias aliasname = type

Suppose that you want to assign a new name to the "Int" data type. This can be done as shown below:

```
typealias MyData = Int
```

In the above case, the compiler was told that "MyData" is the other name for "Int." Consider the next example given below:

```
import Cocoa

typealias MyData = Int

var age: MyData = 34

println(age)
```

Write the above program as it is and then run it. The following output should be observed:

```
34
```

The output shows the value of the variable "age" of "MyData" data type. This is an integer as we had instructed the compiler.

Type Safety

With Swift, type safety is essential. This means that if a particular section of the code is expecting an integer to be passed, then you can't pass a String in place of the integer.

The process of type checking in Swift is done during compilation time since the language is type safe. If there are mismatched types in your code, then flags and errors will be shown. Consider the example given below:

```
import Cocoa

var myVar = 34

myVar = "This is our salutation"

println(myVar)
```

Write the above program as it is written, and then run it. The following output will be observed:

```
main.swift:3:9: error: cannot assign a value of type 'String' to a value of type 'Int'
myVar = "This is our salutation"
```

The above output shows that the program has an error due to failure to obey Type Safety in Swift.

Type Inference

With Type Inference in Swift, the type of a particular value can be deduced automatically during the compilation phase. It looks at the values that you have provided, and then it deduces the type of the values. Consider the example given below:

import Cocoa

// myVar is inferred to be of the type Int

var myVar = 34

println(myVar)

// myVar2 is inferred to be of the type Double

var myVar2 = 5.35179

println(myVar2)

// myVar3 is inferred to be of the type Double

var myVar = 4 + 1.64151

println(myVar3)

Write the above program as it is written, and then run it. The following output will be observed:

```
34
5.35179
5.64151
```

Despite the fact that you have not specified the type for the Data Types, you do not get any error. The output shown above is the expected one, meaning that the program executed correctly. That is how type inference happens.

Chapter 5- Optionals in Swift

Swift introduces the concept of Optionals, which are used for handling the absence of a particular value. They work by saying that, "there is a value, and it is equal to x" or by saying that "there is no value at all." This means that it is a variable on its own and a very powerful enum. It takes only two values, either "None" or "Some(T")" in which the "T" is the value associated with a correct data type that is available in Swift.

Consider the example given below that shows an optional declaration of an integer:

var maybeInt: Int?

An optional declaration of a String looks as follows:

var maybeStr: String?

The above example is the same as a nil declaration, which means that there is no value. This is shown below:

var maybeStr: String? = nil

To understand how Optionals can be used in Swift, consider the example given below:

```
import Cocoa

var ourString:String? = nil

if ourString != nil {

println(ourString)

}else{

println("ourString has a nil value")
```

Write it as it appears, and then run it. The following output will be observed:

```
ourString has a nil value
```

In Objective-C programming languages, Optionals are implemented by using "nil," which has pointers.

Forced Unwrapping

Once a particular variable is declared an optional, if you need to get its value, then you have to unwrap it. Adding an exclamation mark at the end of your variable does this. Consider the example given below:

```
import Cocoa

var ourString:String?

ourString = "Hello, this is Swift!"

if ourString != nil {

println(ourString)

}else{

println("ourString has a nil value")

}
```

Write the above program as it is and then run it. The following output will be observed:

```
Optional("Hello, this is Swift!")
```

However, the correct value of the variable has not been obtained. If this is what is needed, then it can be done as shown below:

```
import Cocoa

var ourString:String?

ourString = "Hello, this is Swift!"

if ourString != nil {

println( ourString! )

}else{

println("ourString has a nil value")

}
```

Write the above program as it is written, and then run it. The following output will be observed:

```
Hello, this is Swift!
```

As shown in the above figure, you now have the correct value of the variable "ourString."

Automatic Unwrapping

Other than the use of a question mark, you can use the exclamation mark for declaration of optional variables. With these Optionals, the unwrapping will be automatic. There will be no need for you to use an exclamation mark at the variable's end.

Consider the example given below:

```
import Cocoa

var ourString:String!

ourString = "Hello, there!"

if ourString != nil {

println(ourString)

}else{

println("ourString has a nil value")

}
```

Write the program as it is written above and then run it. The following output will be observed:

```
Hello, there!
```

Optional Binding

This is used for checking whether an Optional contains a value. If so, the value that is available is made to be a Variable or a Temporary Constant. For the "if" statement, an Optional Binding is always as follows:

if let consName = someOptional {

statements

}

The usage of Optional Binding is demonstrated in the example below:

```
import Cocoa

var ourString:String?

ourString = "Hello, there!"

if let yString = ourString {

println("Your string has - \(yString)")

}else{

println("The String lacks a value")

}
```

Write the program shown above as it is and then run it. The following output will be observed:

```
Your string has - Hello, there!
```

Chapter 6- Constants in Swift

Constants represent values that are constant, meaning that the program cannot change them during the process of execution. Note that Constants can be of any of the basic data types: integer, double, characters, or float. Enumeration Constants also exist.

You work with Constants in the same way you work with the regular values of Variables, but the value of Constants cannot be modified once they are defined.

Declaration of Constants

Before you can use Constants, use the keyword "let" to declare them. The declaration of Constants uses the following syntax:

let constantName = \<initial value\>

Consider the example given below, which shows how Constants can be declared and used in Swift:

import Cocoa

let myConstant = 34

println(myConstant)

Write the above program as it is and then run it. The following output will be observed:

34

Type Annotations

Once the Constant is declared, a Type Annotation can be provided. This will make it clear what type of value the Constant can store.
Type Annotations in Constants takes the following syntax:

var constantName:<data type> = <optional initial value>

Consider the example given below, which shows how Constants can be declared in Swift by use of Type Annotations:

```
import Cocoa

let myConstant = 34

println(myConstant)

let myConstant2:Float = 5.13569

println(myConstant2)
```

Write the above program as it is written and then run it. The following output will be observed:

```
34
5.13569
```

Naming of Constants

A Constants' name can be made up of a letter, underscore, and digits. However, the name must begin with either a letter or an underscore. You need to take care when writing the names of Constants, as Swift is a case sensitive programming language. Simple or Unicode characters can be used for naming Constants. Consider the example given below, which is a valid one:

```
import Cocoa

let _myConstant = "Hello, there!"

println(_myConstant)

let 你好 = "你好世界"

println(你好)
```

Write the above program as it is written and then run it. The following output will be observed:

```
Hello, there!
你好世界
```

How to Print Constants

To print the current value of the Constant or the Variable use
the simple "println" function. To interpolate the value of
Variables, the name should be wrapped in parenthesis and
then use a backslash to escape it before closing the
parenthesis. Consider the example given below, which shows
how this can be done:

import Cocoa

let myConstant = "Population"

let myConstant2 = 2500.00

**println("The value of \(myConstant) is more than
\(myConstant2) thousands")**

Write the above program as it is written and then run it. The
following output will be observed:

```
The value of Population is more than 2500.0 thousands
```

Chapter 7- Operators in Swift

With Operators in Swift, you are able to perform arithmetic and logical operations.

Arithmetic Operations

With Arithmetic Operators in Swift, you are able to perform various mathematical operations. Swift supports numerous arithmetic operators, including the ones for addition, subtraction, multiplication, division, modulus, and others. The language also supports the Increment Operator.
Example:

If the value of variable X is 10 while that of variable Y is 5, then the following operations will give you the following result:

X + Y = 15

X – Y = 5

X * Y = 50

Other operators, which are supported in Swift, include the Comparison Operators, Logical Operators, Bitwise Operators, Range Operators, and Assignment Operators. Note that the concept of Operator Precedence is obeyed in Swift, so you do not have to worry about the order of your operations.

Chapter 8- Decision Making in Swift

With the Decision Making Statements, which are supported in Swift, you are required to specify the test conditions that will be evaluated to know the parts that are to be executed. Some of the statements are to be evaluated once the condition is found to be true, while others are to be evaluated once the condition has been found to be false. There are numerous decision-making statements supported in Swift, and these will form the center of our discussion in this chapter.

The "if" statement

This statement is made up of a Boolean expression followed by a set of one or more statements. The statement takes the following syntax:

if boolean_expression {

/* the statement(s) to be executed if the expression is true */

}

If the Boolean expression is true, then the set of statements that are inside the "if" statement will be executed. If the Boolean expression is false, then the first statement after the closing brace for the Boolean expression will be executed.

Consider the example given below, which shows how this statement can be used:

```
import Cocoa

var myVar:Int = 20;

/* using the "if" statement to check for the status of
the Boolean condition */

if myVar < 50 {

/* The following statement will be printed if the
condition is true */

println("The value of myVar is less than 50");

}

println("The value of variable myVar is \(myVar)");
```

Write the above program as it is written here, and then run it. The following output will be observed:

```
The value of myVar is less than 50
The value of variable myVar is 20
```

The above output shows that our Boolean condition is true. That is why the statement under the Condition was executed.

The "if...else" statement

In this case, the "if" statement is followed by an optional "else" statement that is executed once the condition equals false. The statement takes the following syntax:

if boolean_expression {

/* statement(s) to be executed if the boolean expression is true */

} else {

/* statement(s) to be executed if the boolean expression is false */

}

Consider the example given below showing how the statement can be used:

```
var myVar:Int = 50;

/* using the "if" statement to check the condition of
the Boolean condition*/
if myVar < 30 {

/* statement to be printed if the condition is true */

println("The value of myVar is less than 30");

} else {

/* statement to be printed if the condition is false */

println("The value of myVar is not less than 30");

}

println("The value of variable myVar is \(myVar)");
```

Write the above program as it is written, and then run it. The following output will be observed:

```
The value of myVar is not less than 30
The value of variable myVar is 50
```

From the output shown in the above figure, the Condition for the "if" statement did not equal true. The statement under this was not executed due to this reason. The "else" part was executed, and this explains the source of the output.

The "if...else if...else" statement

This statement is used when multiple Conditions are to be tested. The statement takes the following syntax:

```
if boolean_expression_1 {

/* this will be executed if "boolean_expression_1"
evaluates to true */

} else if boolean_expression_2 {

/* this will be executed if "boolean_expression_2"
evaluates to true */

} else if boolean_expression_3 {

/* this will be executed if "boolean_expression_3"
evaluates to true } else {

/* This will be executed if none of the above Boolean
expressions evaluates to true */

}
```

Consider the following example, which shows how this statement is used:

```swift
import Cocoa

var myVar:Int = 50;

/* use the "if" statement to check for the Boolean
condition */
if myVar == 10 {

/* statement to be printed if the condition is true*/

println("The value of myVar is equal to than 10");

} else if myVar == 20 {

/* statement to be printed if the condition is true */

println("The value of myVar is equal to than 20");

} else {

/* statement to be printed if no condition is true */

println("None of the values was matched");

}

println("The value of variable myVar is \(myVar)");
```

Write the program as it is written, and then run it. The following output will be observed:

```
None of the values was matched
The value of variable myVar is 50
```

As shown in the above figure representing the output, none of the Conditions were met, and this explains the source of the above output.

Nested "if" Statements

The "if...else" statement in Swift can be nested, meaning that the "if" or the "if...else" statement can be written inside another "if" or "if...else" statement. They take the following syntax:

```
if boolean_expression_1 {

/* statement(s) to be executed if the above Boolean
expression is met */

if boolean_expression_2 {

/* statement(s) to be executed if the above Boolean
expression is met */

}

}
```

Consider the example given below, which shows how this can be done:

```
import Cocoa

var myVar:Int = 50;

var myVar2:Int = 100;
```

```
/* using the "if" statement to check the Boolean
condition */

if  myVar == 50 {

/* statement to be printed if the condition is true. */

println("The first condition is true");

if myVar2 == 100 {

/* statement to be printed if the condition is true. */

println("The second condition is true");

}

}

println("The value of variable myVar is \(myVar)");

println("The value of variable myVar2 is
\(myVar2)");
```

Write the above program as it is written, and then run it. The
following output will be observed:

```
The first condition is true
The second condition is true
The value of variable myVar is 50
The value of variable myVar2 is 100
```

The "switch" statement

The execution of the "switch" statement completes immediately once the first case match is found without having to move to the bottom of the statements. In other programming languages such as the C and C++, this is not the case. Consider the syntax given below, which is for the "switch" statement in C and C++:

switch(expression){

case constant-expression :

statement(s);

break; /* this is optional */

case constant-expression :

statement(s);

```
break; /* this is optional */
```

```
/* any number of case statements can be used. */

default : /* this is Optional */

statement(s);

}
```

Note that in the above case, the "break" statement is used. This helps us in getting out of the "case" statements. If they are not used, then all of the "case" statements will be executed. The statement takes the following syntax in Swift:

```
switch expression {

case expression1 :

statement(s)

fallthrough /* this is optional */

case expression2, expression3 :

statement(s)
```

fallthrough /* this is optional */

default : /* this is optional */

statement(s);

}

Notice the use of the "fallthrough" statement in the above syntax. If this is not used, then once a matching case is found, the program will then come out of the switch statement.

Consider the example given below, which shows how this statement can be used:

import Cocoa

var age = 20

switch age {

case 50 :

```
println( "The value of age is 50 ")

case 20,35 :

println( "The value of age is either 20 or 35 ")

case 25  :

println( "The value of age is 25")

default :

println( "The default case")

}
```

Write the above program as it is written, and then run it. The following output will be observed:

```
The value of age is either 20 or 35
```

Consider the second example, which is given below:

```
import Cocoa

var age = 20

switch age {
```

```
case 50 :

println( "The value of age is 50")

fallthrough

case 20,35 :

println( "The value of age is either 20 or 35")

fallthrough

case 10 :

println( "The value of age is 10")

default :

println( "The default case")

}
```

Write the above program as it is written, and then run it. The following output will be observed:

```
The value of age is either 20 or 35
The value of age is 10
```

Chapter 9- Loops in Swift

At some times, you might have a block of code that you need to execute several times in a row. The general setup is that statements should be executed in a sequential manner, meaning the first statement has to be executed, followed by the second, and the sequence continues. There are various loops supported in Swift, and these will form the center of discussion in this chapter.

The "for-in" Loop

This kind of loop is used for iteration over a collection of items such the ones contained in an array, a range of numbers, and a string made up of characters.

The loop takes the following syntax:

for index in var {

statement(s)

}

Consider the example given below, which shows how the loop can be used:

import Cocoa

var myInts:[Int] = [5, 20, 50]

for index in myInts {

println("The value of the index is \(index)")

}

Write the above program as it is written, and then run it. The following output will be observed:

```
The value of the index is 5
The value of the index is 20
The value of the index is 50
```

That is how the loop is used in Swift.

The "for" Loop

With this kind of loop, it is possible to write a block of code that is needs to be executed a specific number of times. It acts as a repetition control structure that you can use to iterate over the set of data. The loop takes the syntax given below:

for init; condition; increment{

statement(s)

}

The "init" is the first one to be executed, and it is executed only once. It allows you to initialize the loop. The "condition" part is evaluated and the execution of the loop is determined by its status. If the condition is true, then the body of the loop will be executed. If it is false, then the body of the loop will not be executed. In the latter case, the execution will jump to the next statement.

With the "increment" part, any Variables contained in the loop will be updated. The execution of the "for" loop will continue as long as the Test Condition is true. However, once the Condition is false, then the execution of the loop will halt.

Consider the example given below, which shows how the loop can be used:

import Cocoa

var myInts:[Int] = [5, 20, 50]

for var index = 0; index < 5; ++index {

println("The value of myInts[\(index)] is \(myInts[index])")

}

Write the above program as it is written, and then run it. The following output will be observed:

```
The value of myInts[0] is 5
The value of myInts[1] is 20
The value of myInts[2] is 50
```

The "while" Loop

In this case, there are the Target Statement and a Test Condition. As long as the Condition is true, then the execution of the loop will continue. The statement takes the following syntax:

while condition

{

statement(s)

}

The statement(s) in this can be single or multiple. When the Condition evaluates to true, the loop will be executed. However, when it is false the execution will jump to the statement immediately after the loop. Consider the example given below, which shows how the loop can be used in Swift:

import Cocoa

var index = 20

while index < 30

{

println("The value of index is \(index)")

index = index + 1

}

Write the program as it is written, and then run it. You will observe the following:

```
The value of index is 20
The value of index is 21
The value of index is 22
The value of index is 23
The value of index is 24
The value of index is 25
The value of index is 26
The value of index is 27
The value of index is 28
The value of index is 29
```

As shown in the output, the last value of the Variable (30) is not included in the output.

The "do...while" Loop

In this case, the Condition is tested at the bottom of the loop unlike at its top as happens with other kinds of loops. The difference between this loop and the "while" loop is that it must be executed at least once. Note that a "while" loop cannot be executed in some cases. The loop takes the following syntax:

do

{

statement(s);

}while(condition);

Note that the Condition is placed at the end of the loop for testing. This means that the Statements within the loop have to be executed once before the execution of the test condition is done. Consider the example given below, which shows how the loop can be implemented:

```
import Cocoa

var index = 20

do{

println( "The value of index is \(index)")

index = index + 1

}while index < 30
```

Write the above program as it is written, and then run it. The following output will be observed:

```
The value of index is 20
The value of index is 21
The value of index is 22
The value of index is 23
The value of index is 24
The value of index is 25
The value of index is 26
The value of index is 27
The value of index is 28
The value of index is 29
```

Chapter 10- Classes in Swift

In Swift, Classes are the building blocks of the Flexible
Constructs. The properties of the Class can also be defined like
what is found in Variables and Constants. With Swift, when
declaring classes, you do not have to define interfaces or the
implementation files, since these are catered for. The
declaration of Classes in Swift is also done in a single file and
after the initialization of Classes. The external interfaces will
be created by default. The definition of Classes in Swift takes
the following syntax:

Class name_of_class {

Definition 1

Definition 2

Definition N

}

The following example demonstrates how a class can be defined in Swift:

```
class employee{

var employeename: String

var age: Int

var salary: Double

}
```

We have defined a Class named "employee" whose properties include the "employeename," "age," and "salary." This is how simply it can be done. If you need to create an instance of a Class, then use the following syntax:

```
let employeerecord = employee()
```

The name of the instance of the Class in this case is "employeerecord." Note that the instance is of type "employee." Consider the example given below:

```
class SalaryStruct {

var salary: Double

init(salary: Double) {

self.salary = salary

}

}

class employeeSalary {

var salary = 600

}

let salary = employeeSalary ()

println("The salary is \(salary.salary)")
```

Write the above program as it is written, and then run it. The following output will be observed:

```
The salary is 600
```

How to access Class Properties as Reference Types

To access the properties of a Class in Swift use the "." syntax. The symbol is used for separation of the name of the Property and the instance of the Class. An example of this is given below:

```
class SalaryStruct {

var salary: Double

init(salary: Double) {

self.salary = salary

}

}

class employeeSalary {

var salary1 = 1000

var salary2 = 2000

var salary3 = 1500

}
```

```
let salary = employeeSalary()

println("Salary1 is \(salary.salary1)")

println("Salary2 is \(salary.salary2)")

println("Salary3 is \(salary.salary3)")
```

Write the above program as it is written, and then run it. The following output will be observed:

```
Salary1 is 1000
Salary2 is 2000
Salary3 is 1500
```

Note that three salaries are defined. Use the syntax mentioned and an instance of the Class to access these, and they form the output as shown above.

Identity Operators for Classes

With Classes in Swift, multiple Constants and Variables point to a single instance. If you need to know the Variables and Constants that are pointing to the instance of the Class use the Identity Operators. Always use a reference to pass the instance of a Class. Consider the example given below, which shows how the Identity Operators can be used in Classes:

```
class MyClass: Equatable {

let ourProperty: String

init(s: String) {

ourProperty = s

}

}

func ==(lhs: MyClass, rhs: MyClass) -> Bool {

return lhs.ourProperty == rhs.ourProperty

}
```

```
let myClass1 = MyClass(s: "Hey")

let myClass2 = MyClass(s: "Hey")

myClass1 === myClass2 // false

println("\(myClass1)")

myClass1 !== myClass2 // true

println("\(myClass2)")
```

Write the above program as it is written, and then run it. The following output will be observed:

```
main.MyClass
main.MyClass
```

Chapter 11- Functions in Swift

A Function is made up of a set of statements that are grouped together to perform a specific task. The Functions are related to those used in C and Objective-C programming languages. Inside function calls are able to pass both local and global parameters. However, you need to know the difference between Function Declaration and Function Definition. In the former case, the compiler is notified of the name of the function, its parameters, and the return type. With the latter case, the body of the Function is provided. In Swift, both the type of parameters and their return type should be provided.

Function Definition

To define a Function in Swift use the keyword "func." After creation of a Function is done, it can take one or several input parameters. These will be processed and finally, you will have the output as the "return types." Use the following syntax to define Functions in Swift:

Syntax:

```
func funcname(Parameters) -> returntype

{

Statement1

Statement2

---

Statement N

return parameters

}
```

Consider the example given below, which demonstrates how this can be done:

```
func employee(name: String) -> String {

return name

}
println(employee("I am an employee"))

println(employee("I like to work hard"))
```

Write the above program, and then run it. You should observe the following:

```
I am an employee
I like to work hard
```

Use the name of the Function to print the text.

Function Calls

Once you have defined the Function, call it, so that it can be executed. Consider the example given below showing how this can be done:

func show(number1: Int) -> Int {

let x = number1

return x

}

println(show(12))

println(show(30))

Write the above program, and then run it. You can choose not to change the program, but write it in the same way it was written. You should observe the following output:

```
12
30
```

Give the Function the name "show," and it only takes a single parameter, i.e. is "number 1," which is of an Integer Data Type. Use this Function to display the values.

Parameters and Return Values

With Swift, the parameters are much flexible. You can also return values that are of either the Simple or Complex Data Types. To access the Function, its parameters have to be passed into the body of the Function. You can also choose to pass either single or multiple parameters to the function. Consider the example given below, which shows how this can be done:

```
func add(number1: Int, number2: Int) -> Int {

return number1+number2

}

println(add(5,7))

println(add(15,7))

println(add(9,51))
```

Write the program as it is written, and then run it. The following output will be observed:

```
12
22
60
```

The output shown above is the sum of the numbers provided to the Function as the parameters.

Other than using parameters in functions, you can also declare some Functions that have no parameters. The following syntax should be followed when doing this:

```
func functionname() -> datatype {

return datatype

}
```

Consider the example given below, which shows how to use a function with no parameter:

```
func employeename() -> String {

return "John"

}
println(employeename())
```

Write the above program without changing anything in it, and then execute it. The following output will be observed:

```
John
```

Functions with Return Values

With Functions, one can choose to return values of various data types such as string, integer, double, float, and others. Consider a situation in which you have an array of integers. You might need to determine the largest or the smallest number in the array. Comparing the successive numbers in the array will do this, and the largest of them will be stored in the area that you have preserved. Consider the example given below, which shows how this can be done:

```
func ls(myArray: [Int]) -> (largeNumber: Int,
smallNumber: Int) {

var lnum = myArray[0]

var snum = myArray[0]

for j in myArray[1..<myArray.count] {

if j < snum {

snum = j

} else if j > lnum {

lnum = j
```

```
    }

    }

    return (lnum, snum)

}

let number = ls([90,11,-10,65,150])

println("The Largest number in the array is:
\(number.largeNumber) and the smallest number is:
\(number.smallNumber)")
```

Write the above program as it is written, and then run it. You
will observe the following:

```
The Largest number in the array is: 150 and the smallest number is: -10
```

What happened? The array was defined and then the numbers
were stored in it. Then a comparison of the values stored was
completed to determine the largest and the smallest values in
the array. The largest and the smallest values in the array have
formed the output as shown in the above figure.

Functions without Return Values

Sometimes, you may choose to use an argument within the function, but the argument will return no value. Consider the example given below, which demonstrates how this can be done:

```
func product(x: Int, y: Int) {

let x = x * y

let y = x - y

println(x, y)

}

product(50, 40)

product(10,5)

product(5,3)
```

Write the program without changing anything in it, and then execute it. The following will be observed:

```
(2000, 1960)
(50, 45)
(15, 12)
```

The Function is named "product" and has two arguments. They were multiplied to get the product, which forms the result.

Using Optional Return Types in Functions

With Swift, a feature named "optional" was introduced. Sometimes, the return type of a value of a function can be declared an integer, but the same function can return a String or Nil-value. In this case, an error will be returned from the compiler. This is why the feature "optional" was introduced to deal with this problem.

Optional functions take either a "nil" or a "value" form. Consider the example given below:


```
func myFunction(myArray: [Int]) -> (minimum: Int, maximum: Int)? {

if myArray.isEmpty { return nil }

var cMinimum = myArray[0]

var cMaximum = myArray[0]

for value in myArray[1..<myArray.count] {

if value < cMinimum {

cMinimum = value

} else if value > cMaximum {

cMaximum = value

}

}

return (cMinimum, cMaximum)

}
```

```
if let bounds = myFunction([9, -7, 3, 207, 4, 89]) {

println("The minimum is \(bounds.minimum) and
the maximum is \(bounds.maximum)")

}
```

Write the above program as it appears, and then run it. The following output will be observed:

```
The minimum is -7 and the maximum is 207
```

As shown in the output above, the minimum and the maximum values were determined, and they form the output.

Local Parameter Names

For the case of local parameter names in a function, these can only be accessed from inside the function. An example of this is given below:

func myFunction(num: Int) {

println(num)

}

In the above case, the parameter "num" that has been declared as an internal variable is accessed internally. Consider the code given below:

func myFunction(num: Int) {

println(num)

}

myFunction(1)

myFunction(2)

myFunction(3)

In the above case, the access to the argument of the function was done externally. After running the program, you will get the following output:

```
1
2
3
```

External Parameter Names

With these in Swift, the purpose of the parameters of a function is made clearer. Consider the example given below:

```
func myFunction(firstArgument x: Int,
secondArgument y: Int) -> Int {

var result = x

for _ in 1..<y {
```

```
    result = result * x

}

println(result)

return result

}

myFunction(firstArgument:10, secondArgument:7)
```

Write the program without changing anything in it, and then execute it. You will observe the following:

10000000

Variadic parameters

Sometimes, the functions that are defined will have multiple parameters. In this case, the members have to be declared as variadic. To define the parameters as variadic use the symbol (...) after the name of the parameter. Consider the example given below, which shows how this can be done:

```
func myFunction<N>(arguments: N...){

for j in arguments {

println(j)

}

}

myFunction(9,10,11)

myFunction(9.6, 12.1, 16.5)

myFunction("Functions", "Variables", "Constants")
```

Write the above program as it appears, and then run it. You will observe the following:

```
9
10
11
9.6
12.1
16.5
Functions
Variables
Constants
```

As shown in the above figure representing the output, the arguments provided to the function form the output.

Chapter 12- Structures in Swift

The use of Structures is supported in Swift. These enable you to create properties, constructs, and methods. They also make sure that the values of variables are not altered. The declaration of Structures in Swift takes the following syntax:

struct myStruct {

Definition 1

Definition 2

Definition N

}

Note that the "struct" keyword was used to declare the Structure. Consider the example given below showing how a Structure can be defined in Swift:

```
struct SalaryStruct{

var salary1: Double

var salary2: Double

var salary3: Double

}
```

To access the members of a particular structure use its name. To create the instances of the structure use the "let" keyword. Consider the example given below:

```
struct employeeSalary {

var salary1 = 1000

var salary2 = 2000

var salary3 = 1500

}
let salary = employeeSalary ()
```

```
println("The salary1 is \(salary.salary1)")

println("The salary2 is \(salary.salary2)")

println("The salary3 is \(salary.salary3)")
```

Write the above program as it appears, and then run it. You will observe the following:

```
The salary1 is 1000
The salary2 is 2000
The salary3 is 1500
```

The data was accessed for the Structure. Consider the next example, which is given below:

```
struct EmployeeSalary {

var salary: Int

init(salary: Int) {

self.salary = salary
```

```
    }

}

var xStruct = EmployeeSalary(salary: 900)

var yStruct = xStruct // xStruct and yStruct are just
two structs having the same value!

yStruct.salary = 800

println(xStruct.salary) // 900

println(yStruct.salary) // 800
```

Write the above program as it appears, and then run it. You
will observe the following:

```
900
800
```

Chapter 13- Inheritance in Swift

Inheritance refers to taking more than one form. In Swift, Classes are allowed to inherit, properties, methods, and functionalities from other Classes. This brings up the concept of the "Sub-class" and the "Super-class." The Class that does the inheriting is referred to as the "Sub-class." The Class from which the methods, properties, and/or functionalities are inherited is the "Super-class." Consider the example given below, which shows how a Sub-class works in Swift:

```
class EmployeeDetails

{

var salary1: Int;

var salary2: Int;

init(year1:Int, performance year2:Int)

{

salary1 = year1;
```

```
salary2 = year2;

}

func print()

{

println("Salary1 is:\(salary1), Salary2:\(salary2)")

}

}

class display : EmployeeDetails

{

init()

{

super.init(year1: 97, performance: 65)

}

}

let salaryobtained = display()

salaryobtained.print()
```

Write the program as it appears, and then run it. You will observe the following:

```
Salary1 is:97, Salary2:65
```

In the above case, the Class "EmployeeDetails" is defined as the Super-class. The Class "display" is used as the Sub-class, and it will inherit the properties that are defined in the Super-class. The "print()" method then prints the salary to the users.

Method Overriding

To do this, use the "override" keyword to inherit the instances that have been inherited and the type methods. Consider the example given below:

```
class myClass {

func print() {

println("This is the super class in our case")

}

}



class myc: myClass {

override func print() {

println("This is the sub class in our case.")

}

}

let classinstance = myClass()
```

classinstance.print()

let classinstance2 = myc()

classinstance2.print()

Again, write the above program as it appears, and then run it. You will observe the following:

```
This is the super class in our case
This is the sub class in our case.
```

Preventing Overriding

Whenever the user does not want the methods, properties, and functionalities of the Super-class to be accessed by other Classes, they have to declare the Class as "final." An example of this is given below:

```
final class MyCircle {

final var radius = 11.5

var area: String {

return "of rectangle for \(radius) "

}

}

class MyRectangle: MyCircle {

var print = 8

override var area: String {

return super.area + " has been overridden as \(print)"

}
```

```
}

let rectangle = MyRectangle()

rectangle.radius = 30.0

rectangle.print = 4

println("The Radius \(rectangle.area)")

class MySquare: MyRectangle {

override var radius: Double {

setting {

print = Int(radius/5.0)+1

}

}

}

let square = MySquare()

square.radius = 50.0

println("The Radius \(square.area)")
```

Once you run the above program, the output will be as follows:

```
main.swift:9:14: error: var overrides a 'final' var
override var area: String {
             ^

main.swift:3:5: note: overridden declaration is here
var area: String {
    ^

main.swift:7:7: error: inheritance from a final class 'MyCircle'
class MyRectangle: MyCircle {
      ^

main.swift:18:14: error: cannot override mutable property with read-only property
override var radius: Double {
             ^

main.swift:2:11: note: attempt to override property here
final var radius = 11.5
          ^

main.swift:19:1: error: use of unresolved identifier 'setting'
setting {
```

As shown in the above figure representing the output, errors
are the result since you are trying to create Sub-classes from a
Class and data types that are declared to be final.

Chapter 14- How to Create an Interactive Notification

iOS 8 brought numerous improvements to the iOS operating system. A new feature named "Notification Actions" was introduced. With this feature, you are able to directly interact with push or local notifications without the opening the application. A good example of this is when a local notification is presented to the user reminding them of a particular task. To handle this, a button can be added to the message to indicate that the task can be done
directly in the notification alert.

Suppose that you need to create a simple counter for the user. In this case, the counter should alert the user after every minute. In this case, the user will be asked to either increment or decrement the value of the counter.

The user can increment the counter by clicking on the "+" symbol or decrement the counter by clicking on the "-" symbol. However, in this case, the project will only be for the local notifications. The notifications in this case are both the local and the push notifications.

Three actions for the counter should be available, i.e., incrementing, decrementing, and resetting the counter. The following code can be used to create the user interface for your app:

//Create the counter actions

// Action for incrementing the counter

let incrementCounter = UIMutableUserNotificationAction()

incrementCounter.identifier = "INCREMENT_ACTION"

incrementCounter.title = "Add +1"

incrementCounter.activationMode = UIUserNotificationActivationMode.Background

```
incrementCounter.authenticationRequired = true

incrementCounter.destructive = false

// Action for decrementing the counter

let decrementCounter =
UIMutableUserNotificationAction()

decrementCounter.identifier = c

decrementCounter.title = "Sub -1"

decrementCounter.activationMode =
UIUserNotificationActivationMode.Background

decrementCounter.authenticationRequired = true

decrementCounter.destructive = false

// Action for resetting the counter

let resetCounter =
UIMutableUserNotificationAction()

resetCounter.identifier = "RESET_ACTION"

resetCounter.title = "Reset"

resetCounter.activationMode =
UIUserNotificationActivationMode.Foreground
```

```
// NOT USED resetCounter.authenticationRequired =
true
```

```
resetCounter.destructive = true
```

As shown in the above code, both the increment and the decrement will be done in steps of "1." The destructive action will lead to a red background for your app.

Your actions are now ready. These actions can be enclosed in a "UIUserNotificationCategory," and then stored in the "UIUserNotificationSettings." To do this, begin by creating a category. The following code is used:

```
// Creating the category
```

```
// Category
```

```
let cCategory = UIMutableUserNotificationCategory()
```

```
cCategory.identifier = "COUNTER_CATEGORY"
```

```
//Set actions for the default context
```

```
cCategory.setActions([incrementCounter,
decrementCounter, resetCounter],
```

forContext:

UIUserNotificationActionContext.Default)

// Setting actions for our minimal context

cCategory.setActions([incrementCounter, decrementCounter],

forContext:

UIUserNotificationActionContext.Minimal)

The category "identofoer" is set since there is a need for you to recognize the category for each of your actions. Used the method "setActions:forContext:" to store your previous actions into the category. Two contexts, i.e., default and minimal have been set.

The minimal context will refer to the notification banner, the pull down notification area, and the lock screen device view. However, note that no more than two notifications can be shown. The default context will only be available when the user accepts to show the notifications for the app as alerts. The following code can be used for building the settings:

// Registering the Notification

let t = UIUserNotificationType.Alert | UIUserNotificationType.Sound

```
let set = UIUserNotificationSettings(forTypes: t,
categories: NSSet(object: counterCategory))
```

```
UIApplication.sharedApplication().registerUserNotif
icationSettings(set)
```

The type of notification that the application needs can be chosen, then settings for passing the types are built, and then all of the categories that were created. Call the function "registerUserNotificationSettings" on your shared application. When you run the above code for the first time, an alert will be presented that will ask permission to allow notifications to be shown.

It is time to schedule notifications. The code for doing this in interactive notifications is similar to the one used for doing this in standard notification, but you have to add a property to point to your category. The code given below can be used for this purpose:

```
let notify = UILocalNotification()
```

```
notify.alertBody = "Hello, just update your counter
<img src="http://www.facebook.com.profile123"
alt=";)" class="wp-smiley"> "
```

```
notify.soundName =
UILocalNotificationDefaultSoundName
```

notify.fireDate = NSDate()

notify.category = "COUNTER_CATEGORY"

notify.repeatInterval =
NSCalendarUnit.CalendarUnitMinute

UIApplication.sharedApplication().scheduleLocalNot
ification(notify)

Handling the Actions

Consider the code given below:

func myApplication(myAapplication: UIApplication,

handleActionWithIdentifier identifier: String?,

forLocalNotification notify: UILocalNotification,

completionHandler: () -> Void) {

// Handling the notification action

if notify.category == "COUNTER_CATEGORY" {

let act:Actions = Actions.fromRaw(identifier!)!

let count = Counter();

```
switch action{

case "INCREMENT_ACTION":

count++

case "DECREMENT_ACTION":

count--

case "RESET_ACTION":

count.currentTotal = 0

}

}

completionHandler()

}
```

The actions are handled. When clicking the "+" symbol, the counter's value will be incremented while clicking the "-"symbol, the counter's value will be decremented. Your app will then be ready for use.

Chapter 15- How to Replicate the Twitter Bird Zoom Start-up Animation

In iOS 8, the Twitter app was changed in that it has an animation that transitions from Default.png to the timeline view. The Twitter bird is used as a window in the animation in the timeline view, and it is zoomed in. The process of replicating the basic animation is easy. A full-blown UITableView is needed. Twitter's logo is also needed. Begin by creating your own empty project. A screen shot can be added to the project as follows:

```
let iView = UIImageView(myFrame: self.window!.myFrame)
iView.image = UIImage(named: "screenshot")

self.window!.addSubview(iView)
```

The next step involves putting the Twitter logo in a new layer by use of the contents property, and then this layer should be used as a mask for the image view. This can be done as follows:

self.myMask = CALayer()

self.myMask!.contents = UIImage(named: "The mask for twitter logo").CGImage

self.myMask!.bounds = CGRect(x: 0, y: 0, width: 110, height: 110)

self.myMask!.anchorPoint = CGPoint(x: 0.5, y: 0.5)

self.myMask!.position = CGPoint(x: imageView.frame.size.width/2, y: iView.frame.size.height/2)

iView.layer.myMask = myMask

The program will now be ready for use. Try to run it, and you will observe that the mask will be setup.

iOS Simulator - iPhone 5s - iPhone 5s / iOS 8...

In the next step, implement an animation for the mask. An observation will be made for the bird trying to reduce in size, and then it will increase in size. You need to do this only once. Use the "CAKeyframeAnimation." The following code can be used for this purpose:

```
let kFAnimation = CAKeyframeAnimation(keyPath: "bounds")

kFAnimation.duration = 1

kFAnimation.timingFunctions = [CAMediaTimingFunction(name: kCAMediaTimingFunctionEaseInEaseOut), CAMediaTimingFunction(name: kCAMediaTimingFunctionEaseInEaseOut)]

let initBounds = NSValue(CGRect: mask!.bounds)

let secBounds = NSValue(CGRect: CGRect(x: 0, y: 0, width: 100, height: 100))

let fBounds = NSValue(CGRect: CGRect(x: 0, y: 0, width: 1450, height: 1450))

kFAnimation.values = [initBounds, secBounds, fBounds]

kFAnimation.keyTimes = [0, 0.3, 1]

self.mask!.addAnimation(kFAnimation, forKey: "bounds")
```

Chapter 16- Swift Protocols

With Protocols in Swift, the blueprints for properties, methods, and other functionalities are provided. It provides a skeleton for methods and properties rather than the implementation. The following is the syntax for Protocols:

protocol SomeProtocol {

// definition of the protocol

}

The declaration of the Class is done after the Class, Structure, or Enumeration name. You can also choose to declare a single or multiple protocols. When defining multiple protocols, a comma should be used to separate them. This is shown below:

struct SomeStructure: Protocol1, Protocol2 {

// definition of the structure

}

To define a protocol for the Super-class, the "super" keyword is used as shown below:

```
class SomeClass: TheSuperclass, Protocol1, Protocol2
{
// defining the class

}
```

Variables are defined by use of the "var" keyword. Consider the example given below:

```
protocol classa {

var marks: Int { get set }

var result: Bool { get }


func attendance() -> String

func markssecured() -> String

}
```

```swift
protocol classb: classa {

    var present: Bool { get set }

    var subject: String { get set }

    var stname: String { get set }

}


class classc: classb {

    var marks = 96

    let result = true

    var present = false

    var subject = "Swift Protocols"

    var stname = "Protocols"


    func attendance() -> String {

        return "The \(stname) has secured 99% attendance"
```

```swift
}

func markssecured() -> String {

return "\(stname) has scored \(marks)"

}

}


let studdet = classc()

studdet.stname = "Swift"

studdet.marks = 98

studdet.markssecured()


println(studdet.marks)

println(studdet.result)

println(studdet.present)

println(studdet.subject)

println(studdet.stname) protocol joba {
```

```
    var salary: Int { get set }

    var performance: Bool { get }

    func availability() -> String

    func salarysecured() -> String

}

protocol jobb: joba {

    var present: Bool { get set }

    var department: String { get set }

    var employeename: String { get set }

}

class jobc: jobb {

    var salary = 96

    let performance = true

    var present = false

    var department = "ICT"

    var employeename = "Protocols"

    func availability() -> String {
```

```swift
    return "The \(employeename) has secured 98%
    availability"

    }

    func salarysecured() -> String {

    return "\(employeename) is paid \(salary)"

    }

}

let employeedet = jobc()

employeedet.employeename = "Swift"

employeedet.salary = 1000

employeedet.salarysecured()

println(employeedet.salary)

println(employeedet.performance)

println(employeedet.present)

println(employeedet.department)

println(employeedet.employeename)
```

Write the above program as it appears, and then run it. The following output will be observed:

```
1000
true
false
ICT
Swift
```

How to Mutate the Method Requirements

Consider the example given below, which demonstrates how this can be done:

protocol months {

mutating func print()

}

enum mon: months{

case january, february, march, april, may, june, july

mutating func print() {

switch self {

```
case january:

self = january

println("January")

case february:

self = february

println("February")

case march:

self = march

println("March")

case april:

self = april

println("April")

case may:

self = may

println("May")

case june:

self = june
```

```
println("June")

default:

println("NO Such Day")

}

}

}

var res = mon.april

res.print()
```

Write the above program as it appears, and then run it. The following output will be observed:

```
April
```

Conclusion

It can be concluded that the iOS 8 brought numerous changes and improvements in the OS. With the release of this version, users can now enjoy downloading new apps for their devices. This is why Swift (a programming language) was introduced. Apple Inc. wrote the programming language, and it lets developers create applications that will run on iOS 8. Due to the numerous functionalities offered by the programming language and the diverse applications that developers can create, there is a need for you to learn how to program in Swift. The programming language is easy to learn and understand.

To program in Swift begin by setting up the programming environment. xCode is the application developers can use to develop iOS 8 applications. To download this application, create an account with the Apple's Developer Website. After that, login to your account, and then download the application. Once the application is downloaded, it can be installed into the system. The language supports the use of Variables and Constants. The use of Functions is also supported in Swift. Decision making statements and flow control, like loops, are supported in Swift.

This means that you are able to create applications with the ability to make decisions in Swift. Structures and Arrays are also supported in Swift, and they act as structures for data storage in the language. The language has its own tokens that can be used to develop your own applications. Hopefully, this book has helped you learn Swift, and now you are able to create your own iOS 8 app.

Thank you!

We would like to thank you for buying this book. Hope you found it helpful in your EASY and FAST programming life development. And we are happy to recommend you some other books from this author:

1. ANDROID PROGRAMMING: Complete Introduction for Beginners -Step By Step Guide How to Create Your Own Android App Easy!

http://www.amazon.com/gp/product/B00WPK68IQ?*Version*=1&*entries*=0

2. ANDROID GAME PROGRAMMING: COMPLETE INTRODUCTION FOR BEGINNERS: STEP BY STEP GUIDE HOW TO CREATE YOUR OWN ANDROID APP EASY!

http://www.amazon.com/gp/product/B011R2H2JQ?*Version*=1&*entries*=0

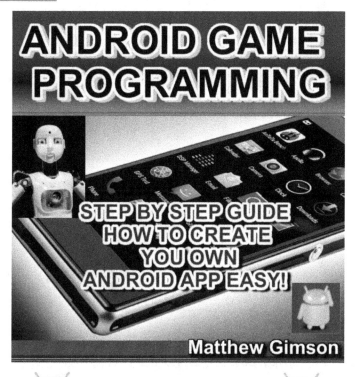

3.   Linux Command Line: FAST and EASY! (Linux Commands, Bash Scripting Tricks, Linux Shell Programming Tips and Bash One-Liners)

http://www.amazon.com/gp/product/B00VPJ100Y?*Version*=1&*entries*=0

4. Linux Command Line: Become a Linux Expert! (Input/Output Redirection, Wildcards, File Security, Processes Managing, Shell Programming Advanced Features, GUI elements, Useful Linux Commands)

http://www.amazon.com/gp/product/B00XGUO4E4?*Version*=1&*entries*=0

5.   PHP and MySQL Programming for Beginners: A Step by Step Course From Zero to Professional

http://www.amazon.com/gp/product/B00XQBYXVW?*Version*=1&*entries*=0

6. Python Programming: Getting started FAST With Learning of Python Programming Basics in No Time.

http://www.amazon.com/gp/product/B00WUNSH6Y?*Version*=1&*entries*=0

**7.   DOCKER: Everything You Need to Know to
Master Docker** (Docker Containers, Linking Containers,
Whalesay Image, Docker Installing on Mac OS X and Windows
OS)

http://www.amazon.com/gp/product/B013X2RPT0?*
Version*=1&*entries*=0

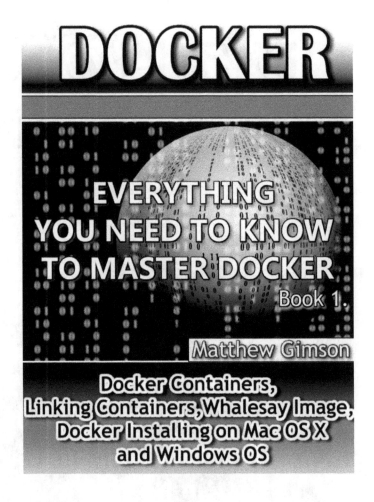

8.   Docker: Docker Guide for Production Environment (Programming is Easy Book 8)

http://www.amazon.com/gp/product/B01452V9IA?*Version*=1&*entries*=0

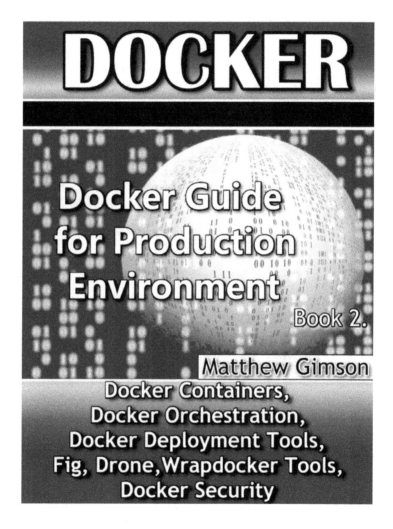

9.   Excel VBA Programming: Learn Excel VBA Programming FAST and EASY! (Programming is Easy Book 9)

http://www.amazon.com/gp/product/B014DIPGVW?*Version*=1&*entries*=0

10. VAGRANT: Make Your Life Easier With VAGRANT. Master VAGRANT FAST and EASY! (Programming is Easy Book 10)

http://www.amazon.com/gp/product/B0151GIRCA?*Version*=1&*entries*=0

11. SCALA PROGRAMMING: Learn Scala Programming FAST and EASY! (Programming is Easy Book 11)

http://www.amazon.com/gp/product/B0151TBXEQ?*Version*=1&*entries*=0

12. NODE. JS: Practical Guide for Beginners (Programming is Easy Book 12)

http://www.amazon.com/gp/product/B01588CXAS?*Version*=1&*entries*=0

www.ingramcontent.com/pod-product-compliance
Lightning Source LLC
Chambersburg PA
CBHW071220050326
40689CB00011B/2386